> "...who brings about peace
> is called the companion of
> God in the work of creation"
>
> JEWISH SAYING

First published in the United Kingdom and Ireland 1994
Christian Aid, PO Box 100, London SE1 7RT

**Christian Aid is a major relief and development
agency, committed to strengthening the poor.
It works where the need is greatest in more than
70 countries worldwide and is the official agency
of 41 British and Irish Churches. With no
overseas staff, it links directly with the poor
through local church and other organisations
which support its own aims of alleviating poverty
by helping communities become self-sufficient.
It also works in the UK and Ireland encouraging
wider support as it seeks to address the root
causes of poverty.**

British Library Cataloguing in Publication Data.
A catalogue record for this book is available from
the British Library.
ISBN 0-904 379-19-1

Printed in the UK by The Beacon Press.

The air over Jerusalem is saturated with prayers and dreams
like the air over industrial cities.
It's hard to breathe...

YEHUDA AMICHAI

AN ELDERLY JEWISH MAN
READS THE SCRIPTURES
NEAR THE WESTERN WALL
IN JERUSALEM.

When as Christians we visit the Holy Land, we take with us our deep religious longings: our personal dreams and hopes, our investment in the stories and promises of the Bible, all the resonances that the holy sites, the landscape and the familiar place names evoke in our hearts. We expect the Bible to come alive, prayer to become more meaningful, God to be more present and vivid to us in the place where Jesus walked.

When we get there, we find a place (particularly in Jerusalem) which is saturated with the prayers and religious longings of many faith traditions. We shall probably see and hear more devout and unselfconscious prayer engaged in, often in public, than anywhere else we have visited. Most pilgrim groups themselves take the opportunity for devotions at holy sites: following the traditional Via Dolorosa, reciting Psalm 88 in the cell where Jesus may have been held (in the church of St Peter in Gallicantu), experiencing a time of silence in a boat in the centre of the Sea of Galilee, and so on. Other people's prayers and liturgies (whether Jewish, Muslim, or of a different Christian tradition), may come across as inspiring and colourful, or as strange and alien, depending on our perceptions. But there is no escaping the intensity of the religious devotion that surrounds us. There is no question that faith will become more vivid as a result of a visit here. But the process is not necessarily comfortable.

To go on pilgrimage is to place ourselves within a very ancient tradition, and it can be a powerful form of prayer. At home, many of us experience prayer as an activity that is begun by withdrawal, taking our body to church or into a quiet place in order to be distant from the complexities and pressures of ordinary life. Pilgrimage is also about withdrawal from our daily preoccupations, going on an actual journey for the sake of our spiritual journey. But that necessarily involves leaving behind our safe, familiar surroundings and immersing ourselves in the anxieties and practicalities of travel, going into situations which are not familiar and may occasionally feel dangerous. We are also accustomed to praying with our eyes shut. Pilgrimage prayer requires us, by contrast, to keep our eyes open. This means noticing not only the sites we have come to see, but what is going on currently for people who live there.

This challenge can be hard to come to terms with. For many of us, a visit to the Holy Land may be the trip of a lifetime which we have saved up for. So we bring with us many of the expectations we bring to a holiday. We are seeking rest and refreshment, and that doesn't normally include having to think about hard things, or experience painful emotions. Also, it is tempting to expect that a pilgrimage will be a 'pure' experience, one that feels 'spiritual' because it is serene and untroubled. I really do not think that anyone coming as a pilgrim to the Holy Land can get through their visit without some mixed feelings – and some of these will be about the role of religious practice, and whether it helps or prevents harmony and reconciliation in the land where Jesus lived.

But this should not make us feel we are 'doing it wrong'. Guide books to the Holy Land will often show shots that look as 'biblical' as possible, selected to omit coaches, souvenir shops, television aerials, the presence of the military or even of an ordinary population in contemporary dress. And tourists often seek to achieve similar snaps to take their pilgrimage experience home with them. But traditionally, pilgrims did not conduct their activities in a way totally separate from the indigenous population. Particularly at Easter, they used to lodge with local Christians and share their worship. Nor did the experience of travel protect them from discomfort by whisking them by air-conditioned coach between hotel and holy site.

Rather than make efforts to filter out our awareness of present politics and daily life (including the somewhat irritating presence of so many tourists just like ourselves), our prayer should look steadily at what is there. For whatever 'contemplation' means, it cannot entail a refusal to contemplate what is before our eyes. If the meaning of why Jesus lived and died is anchored only in the distant events of the past, and within the private, interior thoughts of individual worshippers, then our Christianity is a captive faith, locked into museum sites and isolated souls. It has no purchase on the real world.

This book, through both images and text, makes explicit connections between the biblical resonances of the holy sites which most Christian pilgrims will want to visit, and some of the most pressing issues for inhabitants of the Holy Land today. It has been prepared at a time when a good deal is shifting in the Middle East. The mutual recognition between the Israeli government and the Palestine Liberation Organisation has created the possibility of a genuine peace settlement for the first time this century, and many of us have rejoiced to see it. But peace is not created overnight, especially where there has been enmity, occupation and violence for generations. Nor is peace made through general or abstract good will, but through painstaking negotiation and agreement about just ways of resolving a whole variety of detailed, practical matters that have an impact on everyday life. What this book does is to offer some reflections on peace-making, in relation to very specific matters. Usually the reflections are connected to well-known holy sites, but occasionally prayer is offered in relation to modern sights, like the settlements in the Occupied Territories, which have an important bearing on the peace process or to places like the Yad Vashem holocaust memorial, which no Christian visitor should omit.

Just as the 'holy land' we come to visit has its own pressing contemporary reality, and is not just a vehicle for recalling the biblical past, so as pilgrims we bring our real selves, with the history that has shaped us. British Christians, however hazy they may be about details of Middle East history this century, can hardly miss the fact that their government had a major hand in creating the shape of the conflict which has been so difficult to resolve. None of us are neutral observers, but come with a particular historical perspective which shapes our prayer.

This book is not on its own a guide book to the Holy Land. It does not cover all the sites a pilgrim might hope to visit, nor does it include information such as travel details, opening times and likely weather, or attempt to offer a coherent historical account of the area. For the latter, and for contact addresses for those planning a tour, to enable them to meet local Christians, the CCBI booklet **Holy Land Pilgrimage** is recommended. Otherwise, many excellent and informative guide books, travel diaries etc, are available.

Companions of God simply offers, along with images that connect biblical site and story with modern life, sufficient factual detail with which to pray intelligently. This is included either on the same page as the prayer material, or, in more detail, in the Notes (p. 60). The reflections may be read privately or aloud at the site itself, during evening devotions on the day of a visit, or to enable continued prayer back home when the visit is over. Although the reflections will come alive and make most sense around a visit to the actual place, the images that accompany the texts may enable those who have never been to the Holy Land, yet wish to pray for the emerging peace process, to do so imaginatively. The connections offered are not, of course, the only ones that could be made; the book is intended to suggest a method of prayer rather than to make any final assertions about the meaning of undertaking pilgrimage or praying for peace in the region today.

For many years, Christian Aid has been offering support and funding to non-governmental organisations in Israel and the Occupied Territories, whose work in agricultural and community development, health care, counselling and rehabilitation of the injured, vocational training and human rights campaigns have always been about trying to create the practical conditions for a just peace in the area. Some details of the organisations supported are included in the Notes. They will be at the forefront of developing the new, Palestinian-run local facilities which are planned under the terms of the September 1993 Declaration of Principles. We are publishing **Companions of God** because we believe that praying with understanding is an important part of the active support that Christians can offer at this crucial but vulnerable time of transition. It is an invitation, during your pilgrimage, to stand alongside those who are trying to bring about peace – to become "a companion of God in the work of creation".

Janet Morley, Christian Aid, October 1993

With grateful thanks to the Middle East Council of Churches Ecumenical Travel Office, who arranged my visit in December 1992.

C O N T E N T S

Jesus our brother,

as we dare to follow

in the steps you trod,

be our companion on the way.

May our eyes see

not only the stones that saw you

but the people who walk with you now;

may our feet tread

not only the path of your pain

but the streets of a living city;

may our prayers embrace

not only the memory of your presence

but the flesh and blood who jostle us today.

Bless us, with them, and make us long

to do justice, to love mercy,

and to walk humbly with our God.

Amen.

PILGRIMS WALKING THE ROUTE OF
THE VIA DOLOROSA, JERUSALEM.

What does the Lord require
and to love kindness, and t

MICAH 6:8

f you, but to do justice,

alk humbly with your God?

O God,

I came to your holy land, like Moses to the desert,

seeking a pure encounter,

a cleansing, a pilgrimage,

a new sense of direction.

There are no pure experiences, no unmixed feelings,

no beauty that is not woven with pain.

I wanted truth.

I find several, incompatible truths.

I wanted faith.

I have met faith passionate, intense, real, and blind.

I wanted the Bible to come alive.

I find it living, breathing, and justifying violence.

Yet, like Moses, I do not come innocent to this place.

My hands are also full of blood:

the blood of my country's history –

LEFT: DESERT BETWEEN
JERUSALEM AND JERICHO,
SHOWING THE WADI QELT
RIFT, AND ST GEORGE'S
MONASTERY.

ABOVE RIGHT: BOMBED
POSTBOX FROM THE BRITISH
MANDATE ERA, STILL TO BE
SEEN NEAR THE DAMASCUS
GATE, JERUSALEM.

Britain played a crucial historical role in creating a situation in which lasting peace is so difficult to establish. The Balfour Declaration of 1917 promised both a homeland to the Jews in Palestine and no encroachments on the rights of indigenous populations. Between 1922 and 1948 the British mandate government tried to operate this contradiction, by alternately favouring Jews and Arabs. During the Second World War many Jews desperately fleeing Nazism in Europe were refused entry to Palestine by the British. The ferocious Emergency Regulations that have been used by the Israelis during the Intifada (detention without trial, house demolitions, deportations) were first introduced by the British to combat Jewish terrorism.

our promising of one land to two peoples;

the blood of the holocaust

when Christian nations tried to wipe out Jews.

There is no innocence in prayer,

no innocence in religion,

no innocence in the desert –

just nowhere else to go

to avoid noticing the tenacity of evil,

or carrying my share of history, of present pain,

my share in the struggle for peace.

For, if your disciples keep silent,

these stones will cry aloud.

We beseech you Lord,
who know what the people
of this holy city have
suffered, and are suffering:
uprootedness, lostness, the
pain of being torn apart in
separation, the pain of
unsettlement, the pain
of death.

We beseech you Lord to give this holy city
peace built on justice.

We beseech you Lord to give the people of
this city calm in their souls, and courage
in their hearts.

Strengthen O God the hearts of those who
work to bring justice.

Bless their efforts and make them succeed
over the power of evil, and value and
support them with your Holy Spirit.

NAJWA FARAH, 'A PRAYER FOR JERUSALEM'.

*Ten measures of beauty gave God to the world:
nine to Jerusalem and one to the remainder.
Ten measures of sorrow gave God to the world:
nine to Jerusalem and one to the remainder.*

JEWISH TALMUD

The city of Jerusalem ('Al Quds' in Arabic) is of profound significance to both Israelis and Palestinians, and to the three major religions of Judaism, Islam and Christianity. East Jerusalem was unilaterally annexed by the State of Israel after the 1967 war. Under the terms of the Declaration of Principles, September 1993, Jerusalem's bitterly disputed future will not be discussed until 1995.

DOMINUS FLEVIT

NAJWA FARAH

BACKGROUND: THE
AL-AQSA MOSQUE,
AL-HARAM AL-SHARIF.

ABOVE: WOMAN IN
MUKHMAS, WEST BANK.

Al-Haram al-Sharif (the Temple Mount) has a special
importance for Muslims as a place of prayer at the
heart of their city. Many Palestinian exiles long to be
free to return. Under the Declaration of Principles,
the cases of people who became refugees in the 1967
war will be considered with a view to their return.
No provision has been made for the return of those
who fled in 1948.

Here, where children of the city
at last have space to play,
prayer feels natural.
Beyond the dark interiors, deep and holy,
still flagstones, shade and open sky
compel an easy reverence.
My dusty tourist feet
and Christian soul
are welcome here, but do not dominate.
So here let me remember
those who are not yet free to come
and pray, or play.

"You are my City.
Yet from it I am banished."

NAJWA FARAH

PRAYING AT THE WESTERN ('WAILING') WALL, THE ONLY REMAINING
PART OF THE TEMPLE BUILT BY HEROD THE GREAT IN 20BC.

The very stones cry out.

LUKE 19:40

**Let all dwellers on the earth recognize
and know this basic truth:
We have not come into this world for
the sake of strife and division
(God forbid),
Nor for the sake of hatred and envy,
provocation, and the shedding of blood
(God forbid);
Rather, we have come into the world
in order to recognize and know Thee.
Be Thou blessed forever.**

FROM RABBI NATHAN OF BRATZLAV'S PRAYER FOR PEACE,
BASED ON THE TEACHINGS OF THE HASIDIC LUMINARY
RABBI NACHMAN OF BRATZLAV.

I shall carve my story...

I shall carve my sighs...

From beginning

To end

On the olive tree...

TAWFIQ ZAYYAD

The olive tree has since time immemorial held symbolic power for the inhabitants of the land. Its harvest of oil gives abundance, its blue-grey foliage consoling shade in a bleached landscape. The tree is capable of reaching a great age, conveying a sense of ageless identity with the land it is rooted in. During the period of the Intifada, olive groves were often uprooted by the army for security purposes, and replanted by Palestinians as an act of resistance.

ABOVE: ANCIENT OLIVE TREES (SAID TO BE SEVENTH CENTURY AD), IN THE GARDEN OF GETHSEMANE.

RIGHT: OLIVE-PICKING ON THE WEST BANK.

In the dark shadows
of trees like these
you cried for consolation.
On twisted trunks carved with age
you traced your pain.
Roots like these roots
received your tears.
May the abundant comfort
of ancient trees,
whose arms for you encompassed
all the world's agony,
become today's new harvest
of serenity and peace. *Amen.*

The heart said:
'What have the troubles done to you, homes,
and where are your inhabitants –
have you received news of them?
Here where they used to be, and dream,
and draw their plans for the morrow –
where's the dream and the future now?
And where have they gone?'
The rubble stayed silent.
Nothing spoke but the absence.

FADWA TUQAN

O God,

you bring hope out of emptiness

energy out of fear

new life out of grief and loss.

As Mary returned to mourn

yet found unspeakable joy,

so comfort all who have lost their homes

through persecution, war, exile,

or deliberate destruction.

Give them security, a place to live,

and neighbours they trust

to be, with them,

a new sign of peace to the world. *Amen*.

Nothing but the absence.

FADWA TUQAN

The homes of suspected or convicted Palestinian activists have been regularly demolished by the Israeli military 'for security purposes', under a law originally introduced by the British. It is a practice of 'collective punishment' forbidden by the Geneva convention, and Al Haq, a human rights organisation has campaigned against it vigorously.

ABOVE: DEMOLISHED PALESTINIAN HOME NEAR BEIT UR.

BACKGROUND: ON THE DOOR OF THE GARDEN TOMB ARE
WRITTEN THE WORDS: "HE IS NOT HERE, FOR HE IS RISEN."

He is risen, he i

Is this place holy
because you walked here,
died here,
were raised right here
to bring us life –
or because, in this time, in this world
of trouble and longing and hope
you are alive?
Is this a holy place
because several true churches
have come to fight and worship here,
each hanging separate lamps to burn
for your divided glory?
Or is this land, like all lands, holy,
where people pray, and work,
raise babies and seek justice,
and expect a future?

ABOVE: BAPTISM IN A LOCAL
CHURCH ON THE WEST BANK.

ut here. MARK 16:6

With its rambling and contradictory architecture, and its cacophony of competing liturgies, the Church of the Holy Sepulchre (called by Eastern Christians the Church of the Resurrection) bears witness to the intense inter-church rivalries of Christianity. Six communities share the carefully demarcated territory (including the roof). Meanwhile, away from the holy, disputed sites, the ordinary communities of Palestinian Christians whom foreign pilgrims seldom encounter have shrunk in numbers during the occupation, as people have emigrated to find dignity and work abroad.

ABOVE: WORSHIPPERS JOSTLE TO ENTER THE TINY CHAPEL BUILT OVER THE SITE OF THE HOLY SEPULCHRE.

Who brings about peace
companion of God in the

"For me, participating in Women in Black is part of my Shabbat preparation. Ironically, at the start of the vigil, I stayed away precisely because I feared it would interfere with getting ready for Shabbat. Friday afternoons were dedicated to feverish action in the kitchen.

"How could I have forgotten what Shabbat is really about? It is a celebration of the world as it was in its moment of perfection. Any act one performs for the 'tikun ha-olam', fixing up the world, is an act of Shabbat preparation."

DR VERONIKA WOLF COHEN,
IN WOMEN IN BLACK NATIONAL NEWSLETTER, NO.3, FALL 1992.

is called the
work of creation.

JEWISH SAYING

Ever since the beginning of the Intifada, some Jewish women have dressed in black and stood in France Square in West Jerusalem for an hour each Friday lunchtime, holding banners in English, Hebrew and Arabic saying: END THE OCCUPATION. They have had to put up with insults and harassment from fellow Jews.

WOMEN IN BLACK AT A FRIDAY DEMONSTRATION. THE RED ROSES THEY HOLD ARE BROUGHT EACH WEEK BY AN ANONYMOUS MALE SUPPORTER.

"As we remember the coming of the Christ child, let us be aware that he may not come now in the form of a baby, but as a stranger, a beggar, a member of our family in distress, as an enemy, a soldier, someone who oppresses our people... But these may be hiding the face of Christ. We must offer what is each person's basic need – the need for acceptance, whoever we are and whatever we have done... We have to hold our doors open."

QUAKER MINISTRY SPOKEN AT RAMALLAH, CHRISTMAS 1992.

INSET: CAR WITH YELLOW ISRAELI NUMBER PLATE SET ON FIRE BY INTIFADA ACTIVISTS IN EAST JERUSALEM, DECEMBER 1992.

Enough of blood and tears

> **"It needs time because of the long hardness and killings on both sides. It needs time to understand each other; it needs time to forget our sufferings."**

ADNAN ABU-ZAYED, PLO, JERICHO, OCTOBER 2, 1993.

In the Occupied Territories, Palestinians have suffered routine harassment by the army, restrictions on their movements, detentions, searches and shootings – all the indignities, time-wasting and danger that occupied people constantly endure. Israelis have experienced reprisals in terms of stone-throwing, torching of cars, and ambushes – enduring hostility and danger from those they have occupied. On both sides people have been killed and injured, and families bereaved.

BACKGROUND: ISRAELI SOLDIERS QUESTIONING YOUNG
PALESTINIAN WOMEN AFTER A CLASH WITH SCHOOLCHILDREN

Breathe into these slain, that they may live.

EZEKIEL 37:9

SCULPTURE BY ELSA POLLAK IN THE YAD VASHEM
HOLOCAUST MEMORIAL, JERUSALEM, 'ALL THAT REMAINED...'

O God,

We hear and hear, and do not understand.

We see and see, but do not perceive.

Sharpen our memory,

unlock our grief,

teach us to name what is evil

and refuse it:

even when it seems normal

even when it seems necessary

even when it is commanded by religion;

then, now, always. *Amen.*

FROM ELIE WIESEL AND
ALBERT FRIEDLANDER,
'A LITURGICAL OFFERING
FOR YOM HA-SHOAH'
(DAY OF THE HOLOCAUST),
IN **THE SIX DAYS OF
DESTRUCTION: MEDITATIONS
TOWARDS HOPE**
© PAULIST PRESS.

Whether God is silent

Or weeps,

I will stand firm...

I believe in You,

Even against Your will.

Even if you punish me

For believing in You.

Blessed are the fools

Who shout their faith.

Blessed are the fools

Who go on laughing...

You are mine, with all your wounds.

MAHMOUD DARWISH

Did your feet,

dirty and swollen,

have to pick their way over these smooth stones,

covered with the usual debris

of rainwater and rubbish –

watched by some bored soldiers

who were passing the time of day?

Did your feet,

dirty and swollen,

have to take the long route

right around the road block,

picking their way

past puddles as large as lakes –

watched by some bored soldiers

who were passing the time of day?

BACKGROUND: PART OF THE LITHOSTRATOS, OR ROMAN PAVEMENT, UNDER THE ECCE HOMO CHURCH IN JERUSALEM. JESUS MAY HAVE STOOD THERE DURING HIS TRIAL BEFORE PILATE. THERE ARE SCRATCHED PATTERNS ON THE STONES WHICH ROMAN SOLDIERS USED FOR THEIR DICE GAMES.

ABOVE: SEALED ENTRANCE TO AMARI REFUGEE CAMP ON THE WEST BANK. HUNDREDS OF THOUSANDS OF PALESTINIANS HAVE LIVED AS INTERNAL REFUGEES IN DESPERATELY CROWDED CAMPS WHERE THE ROUGH ROAD SURFACES HAVE OPEN SEWERS.

In this holy land
bricks and mortar have become
not keystones of community
but weapons of occupation;
ploughing an act of resistance
not care for the open soil;
the growth of trees
no sign of shared blessing,
but proof of legal rights.
May all who love this land so fiercely
now build together for peace
with stones that no longer wound,
and work with friendly ploughshares
not forced to act like swords.

As the buildings have gone up... there have been a lot of walls and hatreds building in our hearts and minds.

GEORGE SIRHAN

ABOVE: THIS PALESTINIAN FARMER IS PLOUGHING NEAR THE JEWISH SETTLEMENT OF EFRAT, BUILT ON HIS LAND.

LEFT: OLIVE TREES NEAR JERICHO. THE HILLSIDE HAS BEEN TERRACED TO PREVENT SOIL EROSION.

Over a number of years, Israel has had an extensive programme of settlement building within the Occupied Territories. These towns have been built on Arab land, and they are a major obstacle in negotiating a final peace agreement. To Palestinians, they have constituted unjust occupation of their land. To the settlers, they have represented a religious duty to occupy the whole of biblical Israel. Palestinian farmers have tried to resist confiscation of their land by enclosing fields, terracing hillsides, planting trees, and developing productivity.

Do you want to be healed?

JOHN 5:6

Yes, we want to be healed:

as the dry well longs for water,

as the exile for her home;

as the father wants his children,

and the broken house

demands its people back.

Yes, we want to be healed:

as those who live in fear of the enemy

wish they could breathe safe;

as the fence that divides the village

prefers to be torn down;

as children who dream bad dreams

need an unbroken night;

as those who have long been paralysed

now choose to move.

ABOVE LEFT: SITE OF THE POOL OF
BETHESDA, JERUSALEM, WHERE JESUS
HEALED THE MAN WHO HAD BEEN
PARALYSED FOR 38 YEARS.

The borders and divisions created during various wars have sometimes split families and communities in poignant ways. The reunification of families has often been very hard to achieve for Palestinians, who have had no automatic right of return to the country where they may have been born.

ABOVE: RESIDENTS OF GAZA CALL ACROSS TO THEIR FAMILIES
ON THE OTHER SIDE OF THE BORDER WITH EGYPT.

Yes, worship him,
the God who reveals himself in the cave.

KHALIL HAWI

And this is no surprise;
I have to stoop, as you did
to enter the darkness,
find the warm cave,
kiss the earth,
notice how hard it is.
And at my back
soldiers and souvenir shops –
but this is no surprise;
they had them in your day.
And, in the other cave,
I weep for the slain children
from Herod to the holocaust
(and even to these streets)
whose company you joined.
And this is no surprise.

ABOVE: THE DOOR TO
THE CHURCH OF THE
NATIVITY IN BETHLEHEM
IS SO LOW THAT
EVERYONE HAS TO
STOOP TO ENTER.

LEFT: THE ENTRANCE
TO THE CHURCH OF
THE NATIVITY SEEN
FROM ACROSS MANGER
SQUARE, SHOWING
THE POLICE STATION.

The town where the shepherds first heard the angels' message is proud of its costly witness, by ordinary people, for peace with justice. Very close to one of the sites believed to be 'Shepherds' Fields', a rehabilitation centre is run by the YMCA. Here, young people with disability and emotional trauma from violent injury during the Intifada can begin to rebuild their lives. The director of the centre, Rifat Odeh Kassis, tells this story about the community in Beit Sahour, during one of the most tense times of the Intifada:

RIGHT: A SHEPHERD AND HIS FLOCK
AT BEIT SAHOUR (SHEPHERDS' FIELDS).

ABOVE: PICTURE PAINTED IN THE ART
THERAPY WORKSHOP AT THE YMCA
REHABILITATION CENTRE, BEIT SAHOUR.

Peace on earth to a

"We invited 25 Jewish Israeli families to come and spend the night with us, to share our homes and experiences. Our message was: 'Let us break bread not bones.' The visit was arranged for Friday night so that if the authorities discovered what was going on, nobody could travel back on the Sabbath.

"At 10am the next morning, the Jewish visitors were discovered by Israeli soldiers and told they were in danger, and should leave immediately. They refused. One of the visitors told the soldiers:
'For the first time in years, I slept well because I wasn't worried about Arabs attacking me in my sleep!'"

LUKE 2:1

city at th.

ABOVE LEFT:
PLANTING CITRUS FRUIT
SEEDLINGS FOR DISTRIBUTION
TO VILLAGES NEAR JERICHO.

ABOVE RIGHT:
TEL JERICHO EXCAVATION –
WALL TOWER DATING FROM
THE EIGHTH MILLENIUM BC.
JERICHO IS ONE OF THE
OLDEST CONTINUOUSLY
OCCUPIED SITES OF HUMAN
HABITATION.

Under the Declaration of Principles of September 1993, Jericho, along with the Gaza Strip, is to be the first area within the Occupied Territories to experience a planned withdrawal of Israeli troops and the establishment of Palestinian-run local services. The Palestinian Agricultural Relief Committee plans to plant a million trees to help Arab farmers, who have been pushed onto the least productive areas of land, to improve the soil and to market their produce at a competitive rate.

FAR RIGHT: LUSH VEGETATION IN JERICHO – THE MOUNT
OF THE TEMPTATIONS IS SEEN IN THE BACKGROUND.

City at the desert's end,

city just across the river,

everybody's destination –

you are the land of milk and honey

of date palms and oranges and tourists,

fresh springs and tempting warmth.

Your deepest walls

are older than human memory;

the attacks on you through history

too numerous to recall.

May you emerge

from this, your latest occupation,

friendly and strong and free.

desert's end.

This is your peace:

the water gently slapping on the stones;

soft hills, cool churches,

a sunset to dream about,

that moment of stillness at the lake's heart.

This is your peace:

these waters fairly shared

in a thirsty land –

crops that flourish,

children who drink

without fear of disease –

waters whose sweetness and abundance

are lasting signs of your grace.

Blessed are those who hunger and thirst after

righteousness,

for they shall be satisfied.

Come to the water, all you who are thirsty.

ISAIAH 55:1

The peaceful waters of the Sea of Galilee form a vast natural reservoir. Water is taken in a conduit from here right down to the Negev, in order that the desert should 'blossom as a rose'. How water use is to be controlled and shared is crucial to any final peace agreement. While Palestinian water supplies have been restricted, Israeli farmers and settlers have enjoyed subsidised rates for water, and have used it disproportionately. Overuse is leading to serious problems like the salination of drinking water in Gaza.

ABOVE: BOAT ON
THE SEA OF GALILEE.

The kingdom of God
isn't announced with handshakes
(however momentous),
political flourishes,
or speeches that move the heart.
As in this place,
it will be known
in thorough healing work:
painstaking attention to particular bodies,
committed lives, strategic action;
the binding and silencing of demons
of hatred and injustice
that will not want to leave
or lose their grip –
the mighty works, in daily life,
of flourishing community.

RIGHT: OLIVE PRESS
IN THE COURTYARD
OF THE SYNAGOGUE
AT CAPERNAUM.

What is the kingdom of God like?

LUKE 13:18

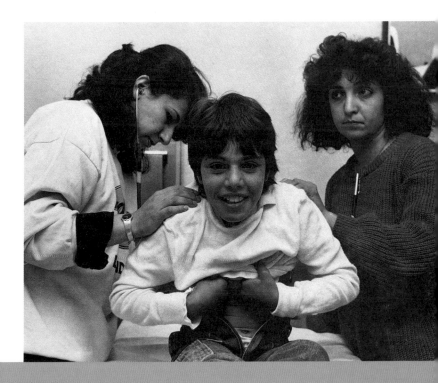

ABOVE: JUMANA AND
MARTA EXAMINE A
CHILD AT A HEALTH
CLINIC RUN BY THE
PALESTINIAN MEDICAL
RELIEF COMMITTEE.

In the Gospels, Capernaum is one of the most well-known places where Jesus healed those who were sick or possessed by demons – doing the 'mighty works' which announced the kingdom of God. Health is still a priority concern today in both Israel and the Occupied Territories, especially for those who work with Arab communities. Access to medical care is poorer for Arabs than it is for Jews.

My spirit exults in God
for he has recognised the humiliatio

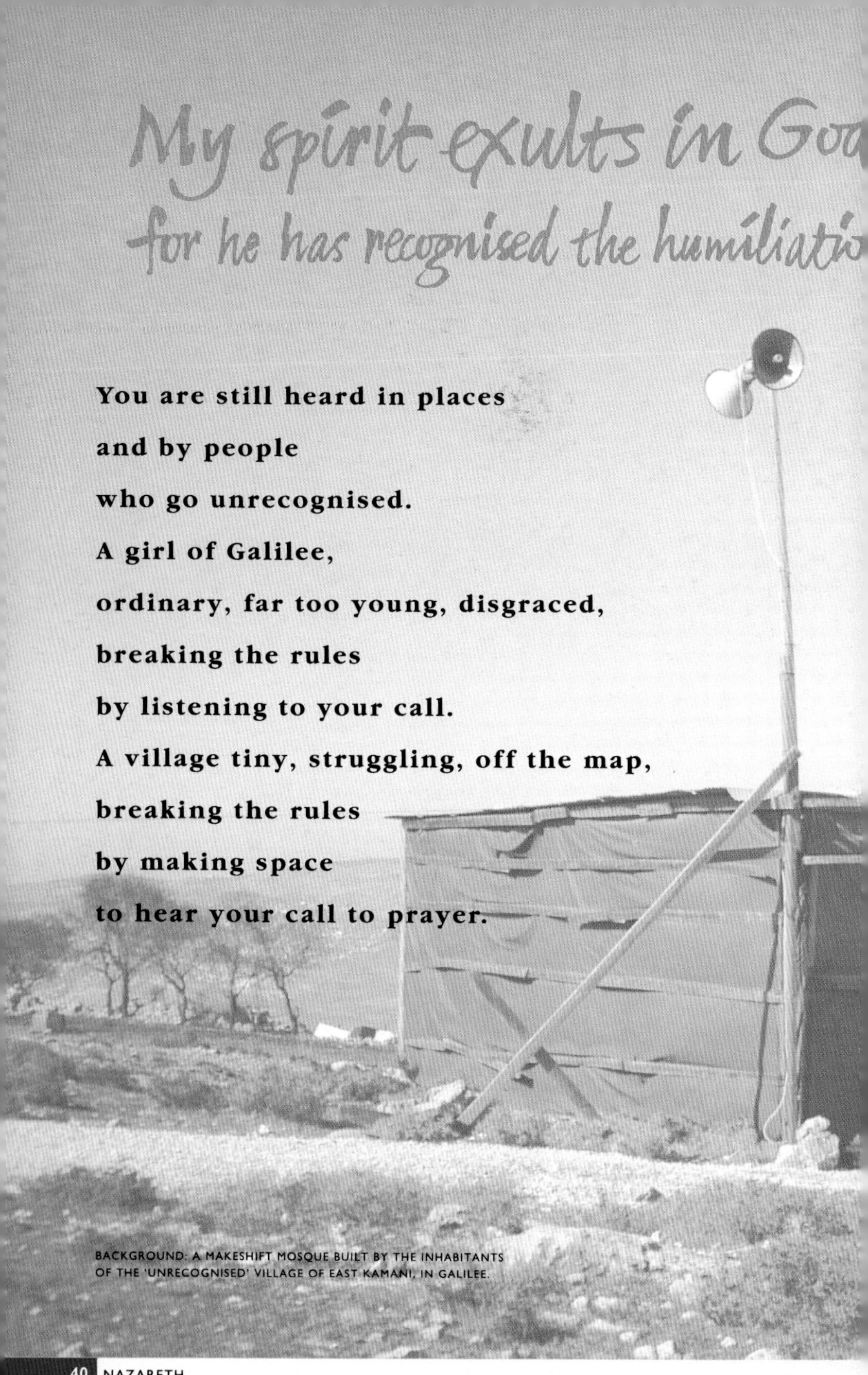

You are still heard in places
and by people
who go unrecognised.
A girl of Galilee,
ordinary, far too young, disgraced,
breaking the rules
by listening to your call.
A village tiny, struggling, off the map,
breaking the rules
by making space
to hear your call to prayer.

BACKGROUND: A MAKESHIFT MOSQUE BUILT BY THE INHABITANTS OF THE 'UNRECOGNISED' VILLAGE OF EAST KAMANI, IN GALILEE.

ny saviour,

his servant.

Among the Arab communities within the 1948
borders of Israel, there are over 70 continuously
inhabited villages that are unrecognised by
the government, and appear on no maps. This
means that they are not eligible for facilities like
electricity, water, sewerage or health care. They
are prevented from building new permanent
structures like houses or mosques, and from
repairing old ones. The Galilee Society runs
health clinics and enables these communities
to press for proper facilities.

ABOVE: MARY'S WELL, INSIDE THE
GREEK ORTHODOX CHURCH IN
NAZARETH, ONE OF THE POSSIBLE
SITES OF THE ANNUNCIATION.

*'God chose what is low and despised in
the world, even things that are not...'*

I CORINTHIANS 1:28

And they all ate, and were satisfied.

MARK 6:42

My people used to plant fields and love life.

Joyfully they dipped their bread in oil.

Fruit and flowers tinted the land

with magnificent hues –

will the seasons ever again

give their gifts to my people?

FADWA TUQAN

The loaves and fishes

placed simply by the altar

feature on everybody's postcard home

(particularly to the vicar).

But no-one told me

about the herons, ducks and cormorants,

that riot across the floor,

nestling in lotus flowers,

stretching their new-found wings,

dancing with snakes,

or sumptuously sipping nectar.

Here in this place of miracle

a wild exuberance

not often found in church.

O God, let loose again this spirit

of pleasure in your world

that we may share and multiply your gifts

and all be satisfied.

RIGHT: FIFTH CENTURY MOSAIC
IN THE CHURCH AT TABGHA,
SHOWING THE BREAD AND FISH
OF CHRIST'S MIRACLE OF FEEDING
THE FIVE THOUSAND.

LEFT: WOMEN BRING THEIR
HOME-GROWN PRODUCE TO
SELL AT THE DAMASCUS GATE,
JERUSALEM.

TABGHA (MULTIPLICATION OF THE LOAVES) 43

Is this the place of baptism,
the place to choose Christ
and turn from evil?
To push past crowds, and coaches,
and other people's lunch boxes
to have the chance to buy
some packaged holiness –
a Jesus-shaped bottle
to put my Jordan water in?
Is this the place?

And yet,
mine is the car park,
I brought the rubbish,
I am the crowd.
I was the one who came here
to purchase peace and quiet
and take it home with me.
O God, teach me to renounce
the evil I brought with me,
and not just spurn bad taste.

m I a passing traveller.

MAHMOUD DARWISH

ABOVE: VIEW OF THE
CAR PARK AT A
PILGRIM BAPTISMAL
SITE ON THE JORDAN,
NEAR DEGANYA.

INSET: MEDIEVAL-STYLE
TILE SHOWING
CRUSADERS, SEEN ON
A HOTEL COFFEE
TABLE ON THE MOUNT
OF OLIVES, JERUSALEM.

The tradition of western pilgrimage to the Holy Land dates back many centuries, but journeys undertaken for the sake of faith have often had a negative impact on the places visited and the people living there. Sometimes faith has been used to justify invasion and violent occupation (1995 is the 900th anniversary of the First Crusade).

Seek peace and pursue it. PSALM 34:14

The desert, with its glaring light

extreme hills

and proximity to death

cannot forget that testament of faith

against all odds.

And yet, what does it mean

to occupy positions we can't leave?

The official Roman army with its might

could not afford to fail:

the desperate freedom fighters

could not afford surrender.

O God, teach us to distinguish

negotiation and betrayal:

when to defend our truth until the end;

and when to climb down

from our embattled certainties

in search of real peace.

After the collapse of the Jewish revolt against the Romans in 70 AD, the almost impregnable stronghold of Masada was the place of a desperate last stand by just under a thousand Jewish rebels. The Roman siege lasted three years, and the men, women and children were found to have chosen to kill each other rather than surrender. This event has become a potent symbol in modern Israel. Young army recruits take their oath of allegiance on the mountain, with the vow, "Masada must not fall again!"

THE ROCK OF MASADA TOWERS
NEARLY 300 METRES ABOVE THE
DEAD SEA SHORE.

A spring of water leaping

Under the gaze of that elusive god,

master of wild beauty and of sudden fear,

where streams of living water are no metaphor,

but rushing past your feet,

you ask the question.

Who am I?

Whom can I trust and work with?

What will be the cost?

O God, just as the Jordan

leaps here to life and runs,

so give your tired people energy

to turn again,

to think fresh thoughts,

and risk a new direction.

Baneas, or Caesarea Philippi, is in the far north of the country, just within the occupied Golan Heights, and very close to the border with Lebanon, the site of so many attacks, counter-attacks, and deportations. It is an area of great natural beauty, which in Jesus' time was dedicated to Pan, the god of nature. In the Gospels, it is the place of a very significant turning point, where Peter recognises Jesus as the Christ.

... to eternal life.

JOHN 4:15

ABOVE: PILGRIMS AT BANEAS (CAESAREA PHILIPPI) CROSSING THE PRINCIPAL SPRING OF THE JORDAN, WHICH QUICKLY BECOMES A FAST-FLOWING RIVER.

LEFT: REMAINS OF THE ROMAN TEMPLE TO PAN, JUST ABOVE THE CAVE WHERE THE SPRING ORIGINALLY ROSE.

This is God's land. We will liv[e]

Women make things grow:

sometimes like the crocus,

surprised by rain, emerging fully grown

from the belly of the earth;

others like the palm tree with

its promise postponed

rising in a slow

deliberate spiral to the sky...

Women make things...

and as we, in separate

worlds, braid

our daughters' hair

in the morning, you and I,

each

humming to herself, suddenly

stops

and hears the

tune of the other.

HANAN MIKHAIL-ASHRAWI, ONE OF THE PALESTINIAN PEACE
NEGOTIATORS. QUOTED IN MECC PERSPECTIVES, MIDDLE EAST
COUNCIL OF CHURCHES, NOS. 9-10, 1991.

n it together
as brothers and sisters.

NAIM ATEEK

PALESTINIAN WOMAN, WEST BANK.

You are my sun at its setting
and my lightened night.

MAHMOUD DARWISH

I watch the sky receive
today's transfiguration;
and vision, glory, hope,
all that this world cannot yet see
is nearly touchable.
And yet, that valley there, Jezreel,
its sheen of beauty biblical in scope,
was once a name of blood,
like Auschwitz, like Shatilla.
And when you met your friends
there on the plain,
no longer bathed in light,
you found them wrestling
with demons they couldn't just dismiss
because they wanted to.
O Jesus, we believe;
help thou our unbelief.

SUNSET OVER THE
PLAIN OF JEZREEL,
SEEN FROM MOUNT
TABOR, POSSIBLE
SITE OF JESUS'
TRANSFIGURATION.

To talk about peace is to ha

"Suddenly there will be a human touch between two peoples. Of course, who knows if it will work?" DAVID GROSSMAN, SEPTEMBER 15, 1993.

LEFT: JEWISH SETTLERS DANCING AT A WEDDING, HEBRON.

BELOW: PALESTINIAN SCHOOLGIRLS AT DAR AL TIFL DANCE DEBKA, JERUSALEM.

"This is a land for two peoples... let's give it a try."

DAOUD KUTTAB, SEPTEMBER 15, 1993.

faith; it is to try for miracles.

GHASSAN RUBEIZ

You have kept the good wine until now;

the wine that we have longed for,

but never thought to taste.

You have taken the tapwater of our lives

our struggles and our ordinariness

and with your grace

made sweet and dark and heady

all that our hearts contain.

So also take the dreams

of both your beloved peoples

in this your holy land,

and make them dance,

that all the world may come

to join in celebration.

ABOVE: WATER JARS IN THE
CRYPT OF A CHURCH AT KAFR
KANA (CANA OF GALILEE).

LEBANON

• Caesarea
  Philippi

GOLAN
HEIGHTS

GALILEE

SYRIA

Capernaum

Tabgha • • Sea of Galilee

• Cana

Nazareth • • Baptism Site

▲ Mt Tabor

Plain of Jezreel

MEDITERRANEAN SEA

River Jordan

WEST BANK

• Tel
  Aviv

• Amman

Jericho •

Jerusalem •

• Bethlehem

ISRAEL

Beit Sahour •

Dead Sea

GAZA STRIP • Gaza

Masada •

JORDAN

SINAI
PENINSULA
(EGYPT)

Negev Desert

l a n d   a n d   p e o p l e

I s r a e l or 'Israel proper' normally refers to the pre-1967
boundaries of the State of Israel (see map), which
was declared after the British left in 1948. Israel was
attacked by surrounding Arab states and the war
resulted in the boundaries shown here. However,
within Israel, it is now illegal to publish a map which
shows these boundaries. Since the six day war in
1967, Israel has occupied the rest of the territory
outlined.

I s r a e l i s About half of Israelis are 'sabras' (born on Israeli
soil). The rest are immigrants from many parts of the
world who have come under Israel's policy of 'aliya' –
the 'right of return' for anyone who can prove they
are Jewish to settle in Israel, wherever they were
born. The main ethnic strands among Jews are the
Ashkenazim (from the US and Europe, including the
former Eastern bloc) and the Sephardim (oriental
Jews). There are also Ethiopian Jews.

Roughly one in seven Israelis are Arabs. The
great majority of these are Muslim, a minority are
Christian, and about ten per cent are Druze or
Bedouin.

The majority of Jews are secular, but religious
practice is strong and has political force. Some
secular Jews are returning to orthodox religious
observance. There are a variety of strands of religious
Judaism, from the Orthodox, some of whom back the
settler movement (see note to pp. 26-27), to Liberal
and Reformed traditions. The ultra-orthodox
Haredim oppose the State of Israel, regarding it as

blasphemous for human beings, rather than the
Messiah, to set up a Jewish state.

Z i o n i s m   The Zionist movement began in the late 19th
century, in response to anti-semitism, particularly at
that time a wave of anti-Jewish pogroms in Tsarist
Russia. Its leading exponent was Theodore Herzl, a
Viennese Jew, and the movement envisaged a Jewish
homeland (not necessarily a Jewish sovereign state).
Palestine was not the only place considered as a
possible 'Land without a People for a People without
a Land' (Uganda was also considered). At that time,
only five per cent of the population of Palestine was
Jewish.

The movement of immigration, which began with
agricultural settlements, received impetus from the
Balfour declaration (see note to pp. 4-5), and, after
the Second World War, from worldwide horror at
the revelations of the European holocaust. Many Jews
see the existence of the State of Israel as the most
important security against any repetition of this. Not
all Jews support Zionism. Some oppose it for reasons
of religious orthodoxy (see note above), others
because they believe that the ethical basis of their
Judaism, or their desire for political justice, is
compromised by Zionist-backed occupation of land.

O c c u p i e d   These are the West Bank, the Gaza Strip, the Golan
T e r r i t o r i e s   Heights and East Jerusalem. The State of Israel
describes itself as 'administering' these territories,
apart from East Jerusalem which it annexed in 1967,
declaring all of Jerusalem to be the capital of Israel.
This annexation has never been internationally
recognised.

Palestine and Palestinians The whole region shown on the map was referred to as Palestine pre-1948, and over the centuries has had many different rulers. Palestinian national self-consciousness has developed alongside Jewish Zionism in this century. Several Palestinian nationalist groups have influence among the population, of which the Palestine Liberation Organisation is the most well-known.

There are about four million Palestinian Arabs worldwide. Most are Muslim, and like many Arab communities, have been influenced by the Islamic revival in recent years. A significant minority are Christian.

Intifada Meaning a 'shaking off', this is the popular Palestinian uprising in the Occupied Territories which began in 1987 and which the PLO called off following the Declaration of Principles in September 1993. It included strikes, non-payment of taxes and other non-violent acts of civil disobedience, along with stone-throwing and more violent tactics like the burning of cars. It began among the Palestinian youth but came to be supported by all ages, following brutal methods used by the Israeli military in efforts to quell subversion.

In September 1993, the Israeli government and the Palestine Liberation Organisation (PLO) officially recognised each other for the first time and signed a Declaration of Principles towards a peace agreement in Washington. The main elements of the agreement are:

In the short term
- Palestinian self-rule for the Gaza Strip and Jericho.
- More limited autonomy for the rest of the West Bank.
- Withdrawal of Israeli troops from the Gaza Strip and Jericho, except that Israeli settlers will still be protected by them.

In the long term
- By early 1996 negotiations will have begun on the structure of a permanent settlement.
- By early 1999 this settlement will come into force.
   In the autumn of 1993, support for the agreement was as follows:
- Palestinians: Three political parties in support, 11 opposed.
   A survey among individuals in the Occupied Territories showed an overall support of 52.8 per cent with the Jericho and Gaza area scoring an approval rate of 75 per cent and 70 per cent respectively.
- Israelis: A poll conducted for the Israeli daily **Yediot Aharonot** showed that 53 per cent of Jews in Israel supported the plan while 45 per cent opposed it. (Source: **The Middle East**, October 1993.)

4-5 On November 2, 1917, Arthur Balfour, the British Secretary of State for Foreign Affairs, wrote to Lord Rothschild: "His Majesty's Government view with favour the establishment in Palestine of a national home for the Jewish people, and will use their best endeavours to facilitate the achievement of this object, it being clearly understood that nothing shall be done which may prejudice the civil and religious rights of the existing non-Jewish communities in Palestine, or the rights and political status enjoyed by Jews in any other country."

   Two years later, Balfour wrote, in a secret memo to the British cabinet: "In Palestine we do not propose even to go through the form of consulting the wishes of the present inhabitants of the country...in short, as far as Palestine is concerned, the Powers have made no statement of fact which is not admittedly wrong, and no declaration which, at least in the letter, they have not always intended to violate." (Source: **The Gun and the Olive Branch**, David Hirst, 1977.)

By contrast, in 1939, the British government published a White Paper severely restricting any future immigration of Jews to Palestine. As a result, when small ships carrying Jewish refugees from Nazi Europe arrived on the coast of Palestine, their occupants were refused entry visas. In some cases, they were deported and interned on Mauritius. In others, the boats sank and many refugees were drowned. The fate of these ships gave impetus to growing Jewish anti-British terrorism. (Source: **Promise and Fulfilment**, Arthur Koestler, 1949.)

In 1945 the British mandate government introduced a series of Defence (Emergency) Regulations, which included the practice of administrative detention (imprisonment without trial for up to six months, indefinitely renewable); the demolition of houses of suspected terrorists; and deportation. These regulations were used against both Jews and Arabs. The regulations were rescinded by the British on the day before their mandate ended in May 1948, but the state of Israel continued to apply these regulations as prevailing local law. (Source: 'Administrative Detention in the Occupied West Bank', Law in the Service of Man/Al Haq Occasional Paper no 1, 1986.)

There has been much abuse of the Bible to legitimate modern policies. Palestinian Christians have found the issue so sensitive that many have ceased to use in their liturgies those parts of the Old Testament that speak of 'Israel'.

6-7   The account of Jesus weeping over the city is found in **Luke 19:41-44**.

Access to the city of Jerusalem has been severely restricted for Palestinians living in the Occupied Territories. During the closure of the Territories for several months in 1993, many who used to travel to the city to work have lost their income, patients and health workers have not had access to Jerusalem hospitals, schools and universities located in East Jerusalem have been inaccessible to their students, and many

Christians and Muslims have been unable to attend worship at their holy sites. (Source: 'News from Within', vol IX, no 9, September 5, 1993, Alternative Information Centre, Jerusalem.)

Both sides have appointed negotiators to discuss Palestinian access to the city, but substantive discussion of its future status will be deferred until the third year of the five-year interim agreement. (Source: **The Guardian**, October 14, 1993.)

8-9 UN Resolution 194 (December 11, 1948), para 11:
"Resolves that the refugees wishing to return to their homes and live at peace with their neighbours should be permitted to do so at the earliest practicable date, and that compensation should be paid for the property of those choosing not to return and for loss of or damage to property which, under principles of international law or in equity, should be made good by the Governments or authorities responsible."

Concerning the return of Palestinians made refugees in 1967, very different estimates of potential numbers have been quoted. The PLO has proposed between 300,000 and 800,000: Israel has proposed 5,000, solely on humanitarian grounds of reuniting families. (Source: **The Guardian**, October 14, 1993.)

12-13 Jesus' agony in the Garden of Gethsemane: **Matthew 26:36-46, Mark 14:32-42, Luke 22:39-46.**

Uprooting of olive trees: The Jerusalem Media and Communications Centre, for example, recorded the details of 2,539 olive trees uprooted by the Israeli military in 24 different incidents during the period January 17-March 31, 1991. (Source: **No Exit**, JMMC, 1991.)

14-15 Resurrection accounts appear in: **Matthew 28, Mark 16, Luke 24, and John 20**.

Regulation 119 (1) of the Defence (Emergency) Regulations 1945 of the British mandate government permitted a military commander to order the destruction of any house from which he believed terrorist activity to have been conducted (without following any judicial procedure), and Israeli military house demolitions have been based on this regulation.

However, under Article 53 of the Fourth Geneva Convention, it is prohibited except in circumstances "where such destruction is rendered absolutely necessary by military operations". The International Committee of the Red Cross has interpreted this to mean "materially indispensable – for the armed forces to engage in action, such as making way for them. This exception to the prohibition cannot justify destruction as a punishment or deterrent." The proclaimed intention of the Israeli military has been to punish and deter. Israeli High Court Judgement 698/85 summarised that "the aim of the regulation is to achieve a deterrent effect". (Source: 'Demolition and Sealing of Houses' Al Haq/Law in the Service of Man Occasional paper no. 5, 1987.)

Al Haq is a legal and human rights organisation whose work is supported by Christian Aid. Fateh Ahmed, one of the lawyers, has said: "You can have the peace of the grave, but nobody wants that. Peace must be predicated on the rule of law."

16-17 There has been a Christian community in the Holy Land since the first century. Formally, the Greek Orthodox Patriarchate in Jerusalem was granted 'independent church' status by the Council of Chalcedon in AD 451. However, the Christian community which once made up 30 per cent of the population of Israel/Palestine is now a minority of only 1.8 per cent. But local Christian churches are glad to welcome visitors. (Source: **Holy Land Pilgrimage**, CCBI, 1992. Please consult this book for details of the Middle East Council of Churches Ecumenical Travel Office, and other contacts for meeting local Christians.)

18-19 For an account of the Creation, with the Sabbath as its crown, see **Genesis 1-2:3**.

20-21 According to the Associated Press, by the last week of November 1992, 106 Jews had been killed in Intifada-related violence, and 982 Arabs killed by Israelis. (Source: **Jerusalem Post**, December 4, 1992.) B'Tselem, the Israeli Center for Human Rights in the Occupied Territories, which is supported by Christian Aid, estimates that in five and a half years of Intifada, 232 Palestinian children aged 16 and under were killed by Israeli security forces. (Source: 'Human Rights Report', vol 1, issue 1, Summer 1993.)

`22-23` In Nazi-occupied Europe during the years leading up to 1945, six million
Jews were systematically murdered, mostly in 21 concentration camps.
One and half million of these were children. Many Gypsies, Slavs,
communists and homosexuals were also targeted for extermination by the
Nazis, but the focus of Nazi ideology was anti-semitism. It is obviously
impossible to do justice to this holocaust in a footnote, and the reader is
advised to explore the extensive literature that seeks to encompass the
events of this time, and to grasp how comparable horrors could be
avoided. Primo Levi's book, **If This is a Man**, is recommended as a way in.

The line "I will stand firm" has been translated by the editor from the
original "ani maamin".

`24-25` Accounts of Jesus' trial before Pilate are found in **Matthew 27:1-26,
Mark 15:1-20, Luke 23:1-25, John 18:28 to 19:16**. It is doubtful
whether Jesus stood on these exact stones. This pavement may not
have been constructed until the second century AD.

There are 28 refugee camps in the Gaza Strip and the West Bank. United
Nations Relief and Works Agency figures for June 30, 1993 identify over
a million people with refugee status (in camps: 456,149; not in camps:
603,380). Living conditions are very difficult with overcrowding, no
proper sewerage and hardly any employment opportunities. Roads have
not been maintained and often become impassable in bad weather. They
have also frequently been blocked by the military authorities to control
access. The camps have borne the brunt of frequent military 24-hour
curfews, sometimes lasting for many days at a time, which have regularly
obstructed the access of residents to health care, food supplies,
educational facilities, electricity, water and telephone lines.

Administrative detention without trial has been extensively used. In
October 1993, when Israel released 700 prisoners, the number of
Palestinians held under this regulation, or serving sentences after
conviction, was estimated at between 10,000 and 14,000. (Source:
Financial Times, October 26, 1993.)

`26-27` International law is unambiguous on issues of land acquisition and
settlement in an occupied territory. Article 43 of the Hague Regulations

of 1907 requires that it be administered, with limited exception, for the benefit of the local population. Article 46 forbids the seizure of property "unless such...seizure be imperatively demanded by the necessities of war." On the question of civilian settlement, Article 49 of the Fourth Geneva Convention states that "the occupying power shall not deport or transfer parts of its own civilian population into the territory it occupies."

Meron Benvenisti, a Jewish historian, estimates that by 1988 Israel controlled half of the land area of Gaza and the West Bank. In addition to expropriating land for military training, Israel has built more than 160 Jewish settlements in the Occupied Territories, taking over land for housing, settlement roads and agriculture. (Source: 'Human Rights Focus', Al Haq, August 20, 1991.)

The Declaration of Principles, September 1993, recognises the anomalous status of these civilian settlements. Although a Palestinian-run police force is planned, the security of Jewish settlers in the Occupied Territories will remain in the hands of the Israeli military.

Organisations such as the International Christian Committee supported by Christian Aid, have assisted Palestinian farmers with land improvement projects which have increased their chance of resisting land confiscation.

28-29 Palestinians resident in the West Bank and Gaza Strip have not had the rights or security which normally pertain to nationality. Their right to reside in the place where they were born can be and in many cases has been withdrawn by the Israeli authorities. Many Palestinian families have become divided over the years, due to the mass flight caused by the 1967 war, and the use of the census in its immediate aftermath to exclude those who fled; to marriages between residents and non-residents; and to the loss of residency rights resulting from temporary travel abroad for work or study purposes. In the great majority of cases, applications for family reunification by Palestinians have been denied. Instead, relatives including spouses and children have only been allowed in on visitors' passports, and are required to leave after three months. (Source: 'The Right to Unite', Al Haq, Occasional paper no. 8, 1990.)

Talks held in the autumn of 1993 suggest that these cases will in future be more favourably considered. (Source: **The Guardian**, October 14, 1993.)

David Grossman (**The Yellow Wind**, Picador, 1988) describes a research study into the dreams of 11-13 year old Jewish children in an Israeli West Bank settlement, and Palestinian children in a refugee camp, conducted by the Hebrew University in Jerusalem. Without exception the dreams each group had about members of the other were conflictual and fearful.

30-31 Accounts of Jesus' birth are found in **Matthew 2:1-12** and **Luke 2:1-20**. Herod's slaughter of the innocents is found in **Matthew 2:13-18**. A chapel to the children is located in the same sequence of caves as that of the place of the nativity under the church.

It is planned that the new Palestinian administration will be based in Bethlehem.

32-33 The account of the angels' appearance to the shepherds is found in **Luke 2:8-20**.

The work of the YMCA rehabilitation centre in Beit Sahour is supported by Christian Aid. It includes trauma counselling and practical vocational retraining especially for those with permanent injury suffered under the Intifada. Disability caused by plastic or live bullets, especially head wounds, can be profound. Employment opportunities for able-bodied young people (let alone for disabled youth) are poor in the Occupied Territories.

34-35 The Bible gives an account of the destruction of Jericho by Joshua's troops in **Joshua 6**. Use of this triumphal account to justify modern occupation owes more to ideology than to historical evidence.

Accounts of Jesus' temptations are found in **Matthew 4:1-11**, and **Luke 4:1-13**.

The Declaration's terms about what constitutes 'Jericho' are not clear. At talks in Taba, Palestinians asked for an area of 395 sq km (Jericho and environs), but the Israelis proposed only 25 sq km (within the municipal boundaries). (Source: **The Independent**, October 14, 1993.)

The Palestinian Agricultural Relief Committee is an organisation supported by Christian Aid.

36-37 About half the farmland inside Israel is irrigated, and the water consumption per head is 404 cubic metres. In the Occupied Territories only 5 per cent of cultivated land is irrigated and consumption is only 130 cubic metres. In the Gaza Strip, according to Mahmoud Okasha at Al-Azhar University, water shortage as a result of Israeli drilling of wells on their side of the border has resulted in dangerous salination of the water supply. (The level of the subterranean aquifer is reduced, allowing sea water to pollute the supply.) This is dangerous for drinking water, and citrus fruit trees, basic to Gaza's economy, are particularly vulnerable to salination. (Source: **The Guardian**, September 30, 1993.) In the Declaration of Principles, article VII provides, in Gaza, for a Water Authority having control over local distribution over the allotment of water it receives, and Annex III of the Declaration provides for a joint committee which may deal with issues of cooperation on water.

Christian Aid supports the work of the Land and Water Establishment for Studies and Legal Services, which studies environmental issues and provides legal help for Palestinian farmers in property violation cases.

38-39 The handshake between Yitzhak Rabin and Yasser Arafat during the signing of the Declaration of Principles on September 13, 1993 in Washington was regarded as historic.

In Israel (not including the Occupied Territories), the infant mortality rate per 1,000 births for 1985-90 was Jews 7.9 and Arabs 14.6 (UK 9.0). A study in 1985 comparing curative and preventive services to eight Arab and eight Jewish communities in Israel found a consistent factor of 2:1 in favour of Jews in all components of the system: doctors, nurses, total staff, and clinics. (Source: **The Israel Equality Monitor**, Adva Center, Tel Aviv, issue no. 2, August 1992.)

The Galilee Society for Health Research and Services, supported by Christian Aid, addresses the numerous health and sanitation problems of Arab villages.

40-41 An account of the Annunciation of the angel to Mary is found in **Luke 1:26-38**. At the time of Jesus, Galilee was regarded with scorn by those living near Jerusalem. (Cf the proverb quoted by Nathanael in **John 1:46**, "Can anything good come out of Nazareth?")

The Israeli Ministry of the Interior refuses to grant formal recognition to some 110 Arab villages. Thus about 50,000 Arab citizens of Israel are outside the parameters of public health care. (Source: **The Israel Equality Monitor**, Adva Centre, Tel Aviv, issue no. 2, August 1992.)

42-43 Accounts of the multiplication of the loaves are found in **Matthew 14:13-21, Matthew 15:32-39, Mark 6: 30-44, Mark 8:1-10, Luke 9:11-17, John 6:5-13.**

44-45 Accounts of Jesus' baptism are found in **Matthew 3, Mark 1:3-8, Luke 3:2-17, John 1:19-28**. The place currently used as a site of pilgrim baptism is unlikely to have been near the place of Jesus' baptism.

48-49 The border with southern Lebanon has for many years been one where sporadic cross-border fighting, rocket fire and bombing has taken place between Palestinian fighters based in refugee camps across the border and the Israeli Defence Forces. In 1982, in an invasion which was criticised by many Jewish Israelis, Israel inflicted a decisive defeat on the PLO. It ended with the massacre mentioned below (note to pp. 52-53). Most recently, it was to the 'security zone' on the border with Lebanon that Israel summarily deported 415 Palestinians in December 1992, who remained there for many months before being allowed to return.

Baneas is just inside the Golan Heights, part of occupied Syria. After years of sporadic fighting between Israeli settlers and Syrian villages on the border, Israeli forces occupied this area during the 1967 war and destroyed over 90 villages. War broke out again during 1973 and part of the Golan (but not the Golan Heights) was returned to Syria.

Accounts of Peter's confession are found in **Matthew 16:13-33, Mark 8:27-33.**

52-53 Accounts of Jesus' transfiguration, and the subsequent failure of his disciples to heal an epileptic boy, are found in **Matthew 17:1-23, Mark 9:2-29, Luke 9:28-43.**

The prophet Hosea, who gave appalling symbolic names to his children, called his eldest son 'Jezreel', recalling the bloodbath there when Jehu brought down the house of Ahab. The land belonging to Naboth, which Ahab had seized, was in Jezreel (**Hosea 2:4-6, 1 Kings 21, 2 Kings 9:17-10:11**). Later, the Assyrians seized territory from Israel in that area.

Hoess, the camp commander of Auschwitz, stated at his postwar trial: "I commanded Auschwitz until December 1, 1943, and estimate that at least 2,500,000 victims were executed and exterminated there by gassing and burning, and at least another half a million succumbed to starvation and disease, making a total dead of about 3,000,000. Apart from 20,000 Russian prisoners of war delivered there by the Wehrmacht, the victims were Jews from Holland, Belgium, France, Poland, Hungary, Czechoslovakia, Greece and other countries." (Source: 'The Holocaust', from Abba Eban's **My People**, Yad Vashem, Jerusalem.)

In 1982 in the Sabra and Shatilla refugee camps on the southern outskirts of Beirut, after the evacuation of PLO fighters, 800 Palestinian civilians were murdered by Lebanese Christian Phalangists in co-ordination with the Israeli Defence Forces, who were in control of West Beirut and allowed them to enter the camps. (Source: Amos Oz, **The Slopes of Lebanon**, Vintage, 1990.)

No sort of comparison is proposed between Auschwitz and Shatilla. But both are place names, like 'Jezreel' in the Bible, which evoke horror and have come in each case to symbolise the tragedy of a people. The memories of the events that occurred in these places and others (with their own separate and distinctive contexts of horror), have a powerful present reality in the hearts of those who struggle now for justice, security and peace.

54-55 The account of the miracle at the wedding in Cana, when Jesus turns water into wine, is found in **John 2:1-11**.

The extracts of poems from **A Mountainous Journey** by Fadwa Tuqan, first published in English by The Women's Press Ltd, 1990, 34 Great Sutton St, London EC1V 0DX, reprinted on pages 14 and 42, are used by permission of The Women's Press Ltd.

Quotations from Najwa Farah, reprinted on pages 6-9 are from 'A Prayer for Jerusalem', in **Palestinian Pain and Promise**, Christians Aware 1990, and from the poems 'Siege' and 'You are my City', in Najwa Farah, **The Colour of Courage**, Christians Aware 1991.

Quotations from the authors Mahmoud Darwish (pages 24, 44 and 52) and Khalil Hawi (page 30) are reprinted from **Modern Arabic Poetry**, ed. Salma Khadra Jayyusi, Columbia University Press, 1987.

The quotation from Tawfiq Zayyad (page 12) is reprinted from **The Palestinian Wedding** trans. A.M. Elmessiri, Three Continents Press 1982.

The quotation from Naim Ateek (page 50) is reprinted from **Justice and Only Justice,** Orbis Books 1989.

i	M. Begg
1	Christian Aid/J. Tordai
2-3	M. Begg
4	Christian Aid/J. Morley
5	M. Begg
6-7	M. Begg
7	Christian Aid/J. Morley
8	Christian Aid/J. Tordai
8-9	M. Begg
10	Le Diascorn/Rapho/Network
12	M. Begg
13	Christian Aid/J. Tordai
14-15	M. Begg
15	Christian Aid/J. Tordai
16	Christian Aid/J. Tordai
17	Alistair Duncan
19	Christian Aid/D. Soutar
20	Christian Aid/J. Morley
20-21	Christian Aid/J. Tordai
22	Nathan Meron/Yad Vashem, The Holocaust Martyrs' and Heroes' Remembrance Authority, The Art Museum
24-25	M. Begg
25	Christian Aid/J. Tordai
26	Christian Aid/J. Tordai
27	Christian Aid/J. Tordai
28	M. Begg
29	Christian Aid/D. Soutar
31	M. Begg (top), Christian Aid/J. Morley (bottom)
32	Christian Aid/J. Morley
32-33	Zev Radovan
34	Christian Aid/Jenny Matthews (left), Christian Aid/J. Morley (right)
35	Christian Aid/J. Tordai
36	Christian Aid/Joan Wakelin
37	M. Begg
38	B. Rees
39	Christian Aid/Jenny Matthews
40-41	Christian Aid/J. Morley
41	B. Rees
42	M. Begg
43	Christian Aid/J. Morley
44	B. Rees
45	Christian Aid/J. Morley
47	M. Begg
48	M. Begg
49	M. Begg
51	Christian Aid/Joan Wakelin
52-53	Christian Aid/J. Morley
54	Christian Aid/J. Tordai (top and bottom)
55	Christian Aid/ J. Morley